THE 12 MOST INFLUENTIAL **MOVIES OF ALL TIME**

by Barbara Krasner

12 STORY LIBRARY

www.12StoryLibrary.com

12-Story Library is an imprint of Bookstaves and Press Room Editions

Produced for 12-Story Library by Red Line Editorial

Photographs ©: George Brich/AP Images, cover, 1; World History Archive/Alamy, 4; NJ Digital Highway, 5; AP Images, 6, 11, 28; DaBler, 7; RKO Radio Pictures/Photofest, 8, 14; Alan Fisher/New York World-Telegram and the Sun Newspaper Photograph Collection/Library of Congress, 9; Everett Collection, 10, 25; MGM/Photofest, 12, 16; Richard Shotwell/Invision/AP Images, 13; Carl Van Cechten/Van Vechten Collection/Library of Congress, 15; Universal Pictures/Photofest, 19, 22; Century Fox/Rex Features/AP Images, 20, 29; Denis Makarenko/Shutterstock Images, 21; Featureflash Photo Agency/Shutterstock Images, 23; Walt Disney/Photofest, 26; Dfree/Shutterstock Images, 27

Library of Congress Cataloging-in-Publication Data

Names: Krasner, Barbara author.

Title: The 12 most influential movies of all times / Barbara Krasner.

Other titles: Twelve most influential movies of all times

Description: Mankato, MN : 12-Story Library, 2017. | Series: The most influential | Includes bibliographical references and index.

Identifiers: LCCN 2016047344 (print) | LCCN 2017005786 (ebook) | ISBN 9781632354105 (hardcover : alk. paper) | ISBN 9781632354815 (pbk. : alk. paper) | ISBN 9781621435334 (hosted e-book)

Subjects: LCSH: Motion pictures--Catalogs--Juvenile literature. | Motion pictures--Plots, themes, etc.--Juvenile literature.

Classification: LCC PN1994.5 .K77 2017 (print) | LCC PN1994.5 (ebook) | DDC 016.79143/75--dc23

LC record available at https://lccn.loc.gov/2016047344

Table of Contents

1 *The Great Train Robbery* Changes Movies

People began making motion pictures in the 1890s. Early films had no sound and were usually only a few minutes long. Rather than telling a story, they focused on showing movement. The films usually featured a single performance, such as an act from a theater or a circus.

That all changed in 1903 when Edwin S. Porter released *The Great Train Robbery*. It told the true story of a robbery

In the movie's eighth shot, the train stops and the outlaws escape.

in which an outlaw named Butch Cassidy and his gang held up a train in Wyoming. Porter's movie showed the whole event. It was the first movie to have a realistic story with a beginning, middle, and end.

The Great Train Robbery was the first action movie.

Porter used new filmmaking methods in *The Great Train Robbery.* Rather than one continuous shot, he used 14 separate shots. He set up the cameras to film the actors at an angle rather than straight on. Porter also used parallel editing. It allowed him to cut between two scenes happening at the same time but in different places.

The Great Train Robbery was the first movie to be a major hit. Its success led business leaders to fund movie studios. They also built many new movie theaters. During the 1900s, movies grew in popularity. Many of them used methods Porter created in *The Great Train Robbery.*

12

Length, in minutes, of *The Great Train Robbery.*

- The movie told the story of a holdup by Butch Cassidy and his gang.
- Filmmaker Edwin S. Porter used new methods to make the movie.
- The popularity of *The Great Train Robbery* helped launch the movie industry.

2 *King Kong* Climbs to the Top of the Box Office

In 1933, *King Kong* gave moviegoers something new. Its special effects brought dinosaurs and a giant ape to life. Before *King Kong*, stories of this type existed only in a person's imagination or in drawings. To see these creatures moving on a movie screen left viewers thrilled and terrified.

In the movie, a group of reporters travel to a jungle in search of Kong, a giant ape. While there, they also discover live dinosaurs. The reporters capture Kong and bring him to New York. Kong escapes and brings fear and destruction to the city.

To show Kong's movements, filmmakers used

King Kong was the first feature movie with an animated lead character.

A dinosaur model used for the stop-motion animation in *King Kong*

stop-motion animation. First, they posed a 22-inch (56-cm) model of Kong. Next, they shot one frame with the movie camera. Then, they moved the Kong model's pose slightly and shot another frame. They repeated this process hundreds of times. When the frames were played one after the next, Kong appeared to be moving.

To make Kong appear 50 feet (15 m) tall, filmmakers layered several shots. It allowed for the movie's most famous scene. In it, Kong climbs the Empire State building while holding a woman in his hand as planes zoom past. This scene required five separate shots: the Kong model, the Empire State Building, the woman, airplanes in flight, and an airplane as Kong grabs it. These special effects inspired movie makers for generations.

6

Number of giant ape models used to film *King Kong*.

- Moviemakers used stop-motion animation to bring Kong to life.
- To make Kong appear huge, filmmakers layered several shots.
- The movie inspired future special effects artists.

3

Snow White Sets the Standard for Animation

For years, people had wanted to add sound to movies. By the 1920s, the technology to make it happen was finally in place. People loved hearing the actors speak instead of reading words on the screen. At this time, an animator named Walt Disney was making short cartoons shown in movie theaters. He wanted to add sound to them, too.

In 1928, Disney released *Steamboat Willie.* It featured Mickey Mouse and was the first cartoon with sound. Excited by his success, Disney took on a bigger project. He wanted to make a full-length animated film with sound. He chose to base it on the fairytale about Snow White.

Snow White made animation appealing to children and adults alike.

Making a full-length animated movie was slow work. Artists had to illustrate each frame of the movie separately. Critics thought Disney was crazy to try such a project. They called it "Disney's Folly." It took hundreds of animators three years to complete the project. *Snow White and the Seven Dwarfs* was released in 1937.

Walt Disney

The 83-minute movie was a blockbuster hit. It was in color, included voices for all the characters, and featured original songs. The music was so popular that it was released as a soundtrack, the first ever for a movie. Disney's *Snow White* set the standard for all animated movies that followed.

ADDING DIMENSION

Before *Snow White*, animation looked flat. Walt Disney improved this in *Snow White*. He had each background layer drawn on a separate piece of glass. The pieces of glass were then layered on top of each other. The camera shot the movie from above, looking down through all the glass plates. The result was a cartoon that appeared three dimensional.

750

Approximate number of animators who worked on *Snow White*.

- Critics thought Disney was a fool to try making such a long animation.
- *Snow White and the Seven Dwarfs* was the first full-length animated movie.
- It was in color, had sound, and resulted in the first-ever movie soundtrack.

4

Gone with the Wind Captivates the Country

In 1936, author Margaret Mitchell wrote *Gone with the Wind*. It was a bestseller and won the Pulitzer Prize in 1937. The book follows the life of Scarlett O'Hara, a wealthy young Southern woman. The US Civil War leaves her poor and alone. As she puts her life back together, O'Hara meets a dashing man named Rhett Butler.

Producer David O. Selznick turned *Gone with the Wind* into a movie. He envisioned a glamorous, full-color epic. Fifteen writers spent months turning Mitchell's long book into a working screenplay. The movie had 50 speaking characters and 2,400 extras. The story also featured sweeping scenes of war, including the burning of Atlanta, Georgia.

Selznick chose to film *Gone with the Wind* in Technicolor. At the time, most movies were in black and white. Technicolor was a new and expensive technology. Only seven color film cameras existed. Selznick used all of them to film *Gone with*

Gone with the Wind's movie poster highlighted the story's drama, romance, and violence.

125

Days spent filming *Gone with the Wind.*

- The movie was based on a bestselling novel.
- It was a major undertaking, featuring sweeping war scenes and period costumes.
- Many people consider *Gone with the Wind* to be one of the best movies of all time.

the Wind. They added life and drama to the story.

Hattie McDaniel

Gone with the Wind was released in 1939. The movie quickly received praise from fans and critics alike. Today, many people consider *Gone with the Wind* one of the greatest movies of all time. It has become a part of American culture. *Gone with the Wind* is still popular more than 75 years after its first showing.

ACADEMY AWARDS

Gone with the Wind was nominated for 13 Academy Awards. No movie had ever received this many nominations before. The movie went on to win eight Academy Awards. One of these went to Hattie McDaniel. The actress played the role of Mammy. McDaniel was the first black person to win an Academy Award.

5

The Wizard of Oz Is the Most-Watched Movie

In 1939, the movie *The Wizard of Oz* opened in theaters. It was based on the book *The Wonderful Wizard of Oz* by L. Frank Baum. The story is about a young girl named Dorothy. The movie begins in black and white as Dorothy is caught in a tornado. A window hits her in the head and knocks her out. Dorothy begins to dream, and the movie shifts to color.

In Dorothy's dream, she is in a land called Oz. There, she meets the Scarecrow, the Tin Man, and the Cowardly Lion. They are each on a quest. The Scarecrow needs a brain. The Tin Man needs a heart. The Cowardly Lion needs courage, and Dorothy needs to get home. They go down the Yellow Brick Road to find

Between 1959 and 1991, *The Wizard of Oz* aired on television at least once each year.

the wizard. They hope he will help them on their quests.

The movie was a modest success when it first came out. Rebroadcasts on television boosted its popularity. According to the Library of Congress, it is the most-watched movie in history. Many of its lines have become common phrases. These include, "There's no place like home," "Lions, and tigers, and bears, oh my!" and "I have a feeling we're not in Kansas anymore."

Queen Latifah starred in 2015's *The Wiz Live!*, a modern retelling of *The Wizard of Oz.*

1,000

Approximate number of costumes used in *The Wizard of Oz.*

- *The Wizard of Oz* is based on a book by L. Frank Baum.
- The movie created two different worlds using color and black-and-white film.
- The lines and songs from *The Wizard of Oz* are part of today's culture.

"SOMEWHERE OVER THE RAINBOW"

The Wizard of Oz featured a new song called "Somewhere Over the Rainbow." Judy Garland, the actress who played Dorothy, sang the song for the movie. In the years since then, hundreds of musicians have recorded their own versions of it. The National Endowment for the Arts and the Recording Industry Association of America named it the number one song of the twentieth century.

6

Citizen Kane Introduces Innovations to Movies

On lists of the greatest movies of all time, one name comes up repeatedly. It is *Citizen Kane*. Orson Welles wrote, produced, and directed it. He also starred in the lead role. Welles had become famous for his work in radio. The movie studio RKO asked Welles to try making a movie. Its executives promised him complete control. The result was *Citizen Kane.*

In this famous scene, Charles Foster Kane makes a speech in his quest to become governor.

The movie begins when Charles Foster Kane is dying. Kane is a rich and powerful businessman who runs newspapers. But he treats people badly and ends up alone. In his dying breath, he utters the word "Rosebud." This puzzles people who know Kane. No one knows what it refers to. The movie traces Kane's life to figure out the meaning of "Rosebud."

Citizen Kane was noted for its innovation, especially the use of deep focus. It is a way to film in which the entire frame is sharply focused.

Orson Welles

It allows viewers to see clues about Rosebud. Welles also chose not to tell the story from beginning to end. Instead, he used flashbacks and flash forwards. He also experimented with camera angles, lighting, and camera lenses.

Like the character Kane, William Randolph Hearst was a wealthy and powerful businessman who owned newspapers. Hearst tried to stop Welles from releasing the film. Hearst thought the film's lead character was based on him. He refused to let Welles advertise the movie in any Hearst-owned newspapers. Hearst also asked movie theaters not to play it. Despite these early difficulties, *Citizen Kane* has become one of the most influential movies of the twentieth century.

THINK ABOUT IT

How could a black-and-white movie with no special effects remain so popular over time? What elements make a movie a classic?

25

Age of Orson Welles when he directed *Citizen Kane.*

- The film consistently tops lists of the greatest movies of all time.
- Orson Welles used innovations such as deep focus and flashbacks.
- William Randolph Hearst tried to prevent the movie from being released.

7

Singin' in the Rain Splashes into Movie History

Between the 1930s and 1950s, musicals became a popular type of movie. They had elaborate singing and dancing routines woven into the story. Many people consider *Singin' in the Rain* to be the best of all the musicals made during these years.

Singin' in the Rain opened in theaters in 1952. It traced the history of movies. The story follows two silent film actors, Don Lockwood and Lina Lamont. The studio they work for asks them to stop making silent movies and begin making movies with sound. This is a problem for Lamont. She looked beautiful on screen but had a screeching voice.

Gene Kelly's famous dance scene took seven days to film, with six hours of fake rain falling on the set each of those days.

Like other musicals, *Singin' in the Rain* had artful dance numbers, catchy music, and big stars.

1927

Year the first movie with sound, *The Jazz Singer,* was released.

- *Singin' in the Rain* highlights the transition from silent movies to talking movies.
- It was one of the first musicals that had a well-developed storyline.
- Gene Kelly's "Singin' in the Rain" dance scene has become one of the most famous in movie history.

But *Singin' in the Rain* also had a well-written, believable story. This was much different from other musicals of the time. Other musicals often had weak plots that served only as a bridge to connect the songs and dances.

Exciting, original choreography also made *Singin' in the Rain* special. In the movie's most famous scene, actor Gene Kelly sings the title song, "Singin' in the Rain." He has fallen in love and refuses to let a rainy night dampen his spirits. He happily sings and tap dances down a rain-drenched street.

More than 60 years after its release, *Singin' in the Rain* still entertains viewers. In 2006, the American Film Institute named *Singin' in the Rain* the number one musical of the past century.

RECYCLING SONGS

Normally, a musical has songs written specifically for it. *Singin' in the Rain* was different. MGM, the studio that made the movie, had many old songs in its vaults. Its executives wanted to use these songs to form a new musical. As a result, 12 of the songs in *Singin' in the Rain* were re-used from previous movies. The only song written specifically for *Singin' in the Rain* was called "Moses Supposes."

8

Jaws Becomes the First Summer Blockbuster

Peter Benchley's 1974 novel *Jaws* told the story of a great white shark. It terrorizes the East Coast resort town of Amity Island. Director Steven Spielberg adapted the novel *Jaws* into a movie. The low-budget thriller hit theaters in June 1975.

At the time, Hollywood considered the summer a slow season. Most summer movies were light, carefree beach movies. *Jaws* changed that idea when it broke all previous records for movie earnings. It quickly became the world's first summer blockbuster.

Viewers loved the movie's suspense. Spielberg emphasized the fear of the unknown in *Jaws*. He used creative methods to increase the movie's suspense, such as filming from the shark's point of view. Composer John Williams wrote a simple, two-note shark theme for the movie. It reminded viewers that disaster was coming, but they could not see it.

Jaws also changed the way movies are marketed and released. At the time, movies opened in large cities first. Then they opened in suburbs

AD LIB ON THE SET OF *JAWS*

The script for *Jaws* was still unfinished when the movie starting shooting. Actors had to ad lib and fill in the blanks. Actor Roy Scheider, who played the role of Martin Brody, made up the line, "You're going to need a bigger boat." It went on to become the most quoted line of the movie.

and rural areas. *Jaws* was released to the entire country at once. *Jaws* also had a new kind of marketing. Two weeks before the movie's release, many ads appeared for it on television. The result was long lines at the theater on opening night.

Jaws left a legacy still felt today. It created the idea of a summer blockbuster movie. Today, studios pour millions of dollars into films to create the best summer blockbuster. *Jaws* began the trend of releasing a film to the entire country at once. Now this is a common practice. *Jaws* also inspired the filming methods, music, and pacing in suspense movies that followed it.

Jaws scared people from swimming in the ocean for years after its release.

1

Number of robotic rubber sharks used in *Jaws*.

- *Jaws* became the first summer blockbuster movie.
- It changed how movies were released and marketed.
- The music in *Jaws* heightened the suspense.

9

Star Wars Transports Movies to a New Galaxy

In 1977, the movie *Star Wars: A New Hope* opened in theaters. Its main character was a young man named Luke Skywalker. Early in the movie, Skywalker finds himself in the middle of a war between planets. Skywalker joins forces with his mentor, two robots, and a pilot. They must rescue Princess Leia and fight the evil Empire.

Critics expected *Star Wars* to flop. At the time, the most popular movies were comedies, dramas, and romances. But *Star Wars* was a science fiction movie. Science fiction had only a small following. The movies were often poorly made stories about aliens or the end of the world. *Star Wars* was different. It was

Star Wars catapulted actors Mark Hamill (left), Carrie Fisher, and Harrison Ford to stardom.

THINK ABOUT IT

What is the appeal of stories about good versus evil? What role do special effects play in a movie's popularity?

George Lucas

a good-versus-evil story with cutting-edge special effects.

This new style of science fiction drew huge crowds to theaters. *Star Wars* was so successful that the film's director, George Lucas, made two sequels, *The Empire Strikes Back* and *Return of the Jedi*. By doing this, Lucas changed how people viewed sequels. In the past, sequels usually only followed one character from movie to movie. In the *Star Wars* series, each movie continued the story where the last movie had left off. This is now a common type of sequel.

Today, *Star Wars* has a secure place in American pop culture. It has generated multiple sequels and prequels. Fans can buy official *Star Wars* lightsabers, action figures, books, puzzles, and videogames. When people refer to the Force, Jedi Knights, or Yoda, they are referencing *Star Wars*.

32

Number of US theaters that showed *Star Wars* upon its release in May 1977.

- *Star Wars* changed the way people thought about science fiction movies.
- The *Star Wars* series made sequels more common.
- *Star Wars* has become part of American pop culture.

10

Jurassic Park's Special Effects Thrill Audiences

Jurassic Park began as a bestselling book by Michael Crichton in 1990. It tracks scientists who have discovered how to clone dinosaurs. They do their experiments on a remote island. The scientists working there must figure out how to survive among the newly created dinosaurs.

Director Steven Spielberg turned *Jurassic Park* into a blockbuster movie in 1993. One of the movie's biggest challenges was showing dinosaurs that looked real. In the past, moviemakers had to rely on stop-motion animation for this. But this method often looked jerky. Viewers knew they were looking at something fake.

Spielberg wanted to make the dinosaurs look real. To do it, he used computer-generated imagery (CGI). CGI allowed the dinosaurs to have smooth movements and realistic skin, eyes, and claws. Spielberg combined the CGI dinosaurs with life-size dinosaur models. Then he

Jurassic Park inspired the widespread use of CGI in movies.

layered footage of the dinosaurs and actors together.

Spielberg also wanted the dinosaurs to sound real. So the sound crew recorded donkeys, dogs, cows, elephants, and tortoises. Then they edited and slowed down the sounds. Spielberg had the sounds recoded digitally on a system called DTS. It was the first movie to use DTS. The result was realistic sounds that made it seem as if the dinosaurs were in the theater.

Jurassic Park's CGI and digital sound left audiences scared, amazed, and awed. Never had a movie with special effects seemed so real. The CGI and digital sound recordings Spielberg pioneered became a model for future movies.

4

Number of minutes of CGI dinosaur footage in *Jurassic Park*.

- Steven Spielberg used CGI to create realistic-looking dinosaurs.
- To make the sounds real, Spielberg used digital recordings.
- *Jurassic Park* was a pioneer in realistic special effects that are still used today.

Steven Spielberg

11

Toy Story Updates Animation

In 1991, Pixar and Disney joined together for a project. They wanted to make the world's first full-length movie using only computer animation. Many critics doubted it could be done. The technology to create this type of movie did not yet exist. Animators pushed forward despite the doubts.

Making *Toy Story* required creativity and patience. Animators worked with programmers to invent new software. One type of software was for rigging. It allowed animators to give realistic movements to computer-created characters. While the animators were focused on technology, they were careful not to let it take over. They did not want the technology to distract viewers from the story.

The result of all the hard work was 1995's blockbuster movie *Toy Story*. In the movie, six-year-old Andy's toys come to life when he is not in the room. One of them, a cowboy named Woody, is unhappy when Andy receives a new toy for his birthday. The new toy, an astronaut named Buzz Lightyear, must defend himself against Woody and the other toys. The movie became an instant classic.

Toy Story had achieved what many people thought was impossible.

27

Number of animators who worked on *Toy Story*.

- *Toy Story* was the first full-length movie animated completely by computers.
- The *Toy Story* team invented software to make computer animation possible.
- Animators worked to make sure the new technology did not overshadow the story.

This pioneering work was recognized with three Academy Awards. The *Toy Story* team also won a special award for the most significant animation achievement since the introduction of color. *Toy Story* ushered in a new era in animation. Since *Toy Story*'s creation, more than 250 movies have been made using computer animation.

In *Toy Story*, the characters Woody and Buzz Lightyear compete for the affection of their owner, Andy.

12

Frozen Blows Audiences Away

Beginning with *Snow White* in 1937, Disney earned a reputation for its princess movies. *Cinderella*, *Beauty and the Beast*, and *Sleeping Beauty* have become classics. But critics have wondered whether princess movies are good for girls. The princesses often rely on their looks rather than their intelligence or courage. Instead of solving their own problems, the princesses depend upon princes to do it for them.

In response, Disney began making movies with princesses who broke this stereotype. Rapunzel from

Frozen was loosely based on "The Snow Queen," a fairy tale by Hans Christian Andersen.

Tangled and Merida from *Brave* both fought against the ideas of weak female princesses. But Disney's greatest success with a new type of princess came in 2013. That year, Disney released the movie *Frozen.*

Frozen tells the story of two princesses, Elsa and Anna. As in past princess movies, Elsa and Anna rely on love to solve their problems. But in this case, it is love between sisters rather than love between a princess and prince. Elsa and Anna face their problems with bravery, intelligence, and humor. Audiences loved Elsa and Anna and flocked to theaters to watch them.

Frozen had other elements that made it successful, too. It boasted beautiful animation, with an icy, snowy world that dazzled viewers. Its most famous song, "Let It Go," had children across the country singing along. It later won the Academy Award for Best Original Song. These elements combined to make *Frozen* the highest-earning animated movie in history.

Actress Idina Menzel provided the voice for Elsa in *Frozen.*

41

Number of languages into which *Frozen* has been translated.

- In the past, Disney movies made princesses rely upon their looks and their princes.
- *Frozen* focused on the love between sisters.
- The award-winning songs in *Frozen* boosted the movie's popularity.

Other Notable Movies

Who Framed Roger Rabbit

Released in 1988, this movie combines live action and animation. A detective is hired to check into the activities of a movie studio's film star—cartoon character Jessica Rabbit, the wife of jumpy Roger.

The Little Mermaid

This 1989 animation featured a rebellious mermaid named Ariel. It gave Disney Studios its first hit movie in 30 years.

Titanic

Titanic tells the story of the ship's doomed maiden voyage. The combination of realistic special effects, romance, and disaster made its actors stars and its soundtrack a bestseller.

The Lord of the Rings

This trio of movies is adapted from the work of writer J. R. R. Tolkien. Like *Star Wars*, this is a story of a hero's quest to battle evil. The films received nominations for 30 Academy Awards.

Avatar

Avatar is a 3-D movie that redefined what viewers could expect when they go to the movies, much like sound in the 1920s and color in the 1930s. The story takes place in the twenty-second century on a mining outpost planet named Pandora.

Glossary

ad lib
To speak without having words prepared in advance.

blockbuster
A movie that has broad audience appeal and financial success.

epic
A long book, poem, or movie that recounts legendary events of the past.

extra
A person who has a nonspeaking role in a movie or play.

footage
The content contained in a specific section of a movie's film.

frame
One of many still images that form a movie.

screenplay
The outline or manuscript for a motion picture.

shot
Several frames in a movie that make up a scene.

soundtrack
A recording of the songs from a movie.

stereotype
An overly simplified belief that all people within a certain group are the same.

For More Information

Books

Clark, Steven B. and Rebecca Cline. *The Walt Disney Studio: A Lot to Remember.* Glendale, CA: Disney Editions, 2016.

Smith, Ian Haydn. *1001 Movies You Must See Before You Die.* New York: Barron's Educational Series, 2015.

Visit 12StoryLibrary.com

Scan the code or use your school's login at **12StoryLibrary.com** for recent updates about this topic and a full digital version of this book. Enjoy free access to:

- Digital ebook
- Breaking news updates
- Live content feeds
- Videos, interactive maps, and graphics
- Additional web resources

Note to educators: Visit 12StoryLibrary.com/register to sign up for free premium website access. Enjoy live content plus a full digital version of every 12-Story Library book you own for every student at your school.

Editor's note: The 12 topics featured in this book are selected by the author and approved by the book's editor. While not a definitive list, the selected topics are an attempt to balance the book's subject with the intended readership. To expand learning about this subject, please visit **12StoryLibrary.com** or use this book's QR code to access free additional content.

Index

About the Author

Barbara Krasner has been an enthusiastic movie buff since she saw her first film, *Snow White and the Seven Dwarfs*. She holds a master's degree in writing for children and teaches children's literature and creative writing. She is the author of more than 15 books for young readers.